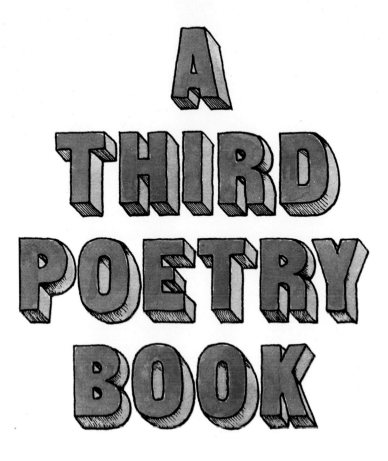

A THIRD POETRY BOOK

compiled by John Foster

illustrated by
Allan Curless
Michael McManus
John Raynes

Oxford University Press

Oxford University Press, Walton Street, Oxford OX2 6DP

Oxford New York Toronto
Delhi Bombay Calcutta Madras Karachi
Petaling Jaya Singapore Hong Kong Tokyo
Nairobi Dar es Salaam Cape Town
Melbourne Auckland

and associated companies in
Berlin Ibadan

Oxford is a trade mark of Oxford University Press

First published 1982
Reprinted 1983, 1984, 1985, 1986, 1987, 1988

ISBN 0 19 918139 X (paperback)
ISBN 0 19 918140 3 (hardback)

Composition in Palatino by Filmtype Services Limited, Scarborough, North Yorkshire
Printed in Hong Kong

Contents

The Mystery Creatures

They dwell on a planet not far
  from the Sun.
Some fly through the sky, while
  others just run.
Some have big heads which are
  hairless as tin,
while others have hair which
  sprouts from their skin.
They dig food from dirt, and
  gobble dead meat.
The young squeal like pigs if you
  tickle their feet.
They slurp, burp, and grunt;
  their manners are bad.
Their eyes become waterfalls
  When they feel sad.
Well, who are these creatures?
  Can you guess who?
The answer is easy: it's you,
  you, and YOU.

Wes Magee

The Alien

The alien
Was as round as the moon.
Five legs he had
And his ears played a tune.
His hair was pink
And his knees were green,
He was the funniest thing I'd seen
As he danced in the door
Of his strange spacecraft,
He looked at me —
And laughed and laughed!

Julie Holder

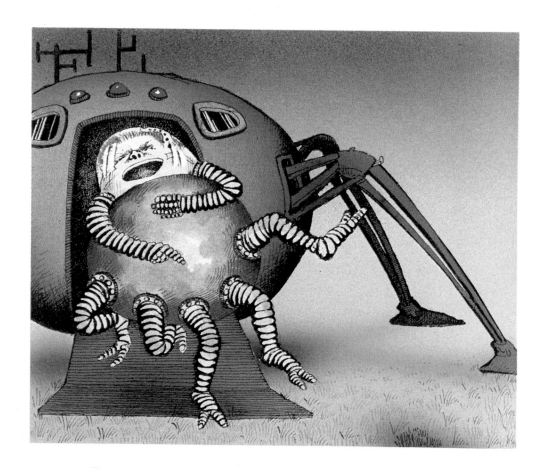

Mr Ah Choo

Mr Ah Choo was Chinese.
He came to Europe from Peking.
He was a man of many talents:
He could skip, he could dance, he could sing.
He wasn't very tall,
But he was very polite,
And whenever a stranger came into sight
Mr Ah Choo raised his hat,
Smiled, bowed — but after that
It was always the same,
When he told them his name,
They didn't say, 'Hello, how do you do?'
All they said was, 'Bless you! Bless you!'

Now when *you* meet Mr Ah Choo, please don't tease.
Remember: he isn't a sneeze. He's simply Chinese.

Gyles Brandreth

9

Reflection

In the oval mirror
I see my face reflected.

'Hullo,' I say to the mirror
'you're wearing a fine suit.

You're wearing a nice wristwatch
and shoes that are well polished.

Where are you going today?
Can I come with you?'

Iain Crichton Smith

10

Eager and Stout

There was an old gentleman
eager and stout
who wondered whatever
the world was about.

On Tuesdays and Wednesdays,
on Sundays and Sat
he asked all his neighbours
'Pray, what are you AT?'

And some of them cried
'We are shining our shoes!'
Or 'We're peeling potatoes!'
Or 'Reading the news!

But WHY it is so
we can't possibly tell.
Why don't YOU make haste
and be busy as well?'

But this misty old gentleman
(eager and stout)
murmured 'Certainly not!
What's the bustle about?'

And he went away silently
scratching his head.
'I wonder ...
    I wonder ...
        I wonder ...'
            he said.

Jean Kenward

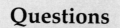

Questions

What is ... a Million?

The blades of grass growing on your back lawn.
The people you've met since the day you were born.

The age of a fossil you found by the sea.
The years it would take you to reach Octran Three.

The words you have read since you started school.
The water drops needed to fill the fish pool.

The postcards sent in to *Record Requests*.
The hairs that are growing on your dad's chest.

What is ... the Sun?

The sun is an orange dinghy
   sailing across a calm sea.

It is a gold coin
   dropped down a drain in heaven.

It is a yellow beach ball
   kicked high into the summer sky.

It is a red thumb-print
   on a sheet of pale blue paper.

It is the gold top from a milk bottle
   floating on a puddle.

Wes Magee

Why is it?

Why is it,
That,
In our bathroom,
It's not the dirtiest
Or the strongest
Who stays longest?
BUT
It always seems to be
The one who gets there
Just ahead
Of me.

Why is it
That people fret
When they're wet,
With loud cries
And soap in their eyes
And agonized howls,
Because they forget
Their towels?

Why is it that —
When *I'm* in the bath,
Steaming and dreaming,
My toes just showing
And the hot water flowing,
That other people
Yell and say,
'Are you there to stay
Or just on a visit?'

Why is it?

Max Fatchen

14

Soap

New cakes of soap
have names you can feel —
letters that stand up under fingers
like ears, lips, eyelids
on a soft face.

Old cakes of soap
are as smooth to stroke
as a chin.

Judith Thurman

15

If your hands get wet

If your hands get wet
in the washing-up water,
if they get covered in flour
if you get grease or oil
all over your fingers
if they land up in the mud,
wet grit, paint, or glue . . .

have you noticed
it's just then
that you always get
a terrible itch
just inside your nose?
and you can try and twitch your nose,
twist your nose,
squeeze your nose
scratch it with your arm
scrape your nose on your shoulder
or press it up against the wall
but it's no good.
You can't get rid of the itch.
It drives you so mad
you just *have* to let a finger get at it.
And before you know you've done it,
you've wiped a load of glue,
or oil,
or cold wet pastry
all over the end of your nose.

Michael Rosen

Once I was round a friend's place

Once I was round a friend's place
and just as we were going out
he went over to the table
and picked a hard lump of chewed-up
chewing gum with teeth marks in it
off the table top
and stuffed it in his mouth.

His gran was there and she said,
'You're not taking that filthy thing
with you, are you?'
And he said to me,
'Quick — let's get out of here.'

Michael Rosen

Give up slimming, Mum

My mum
is short
and plump
and pretty
and I wish
she'd give up
slimming.

So does Dad.

Her cooking's
delicious —
you can't
beat it —
but you really can
hardly bear
to eat it —
the way she sits
with her eyes
brimming,
watching you
polish off
the spuds
and trimmings
while she
has nothing
herself but a small
thin dry
diet biscuit;
that's all.

My mum
is short
and plump
and pretty
and I wish
she'd give up
slimming.

So does Dad.

She says she
looks as though
someone had
sat on her —
BUT WE LIKE MUM
WITH A BIT
OF FAT ON HER!

Kit Wright

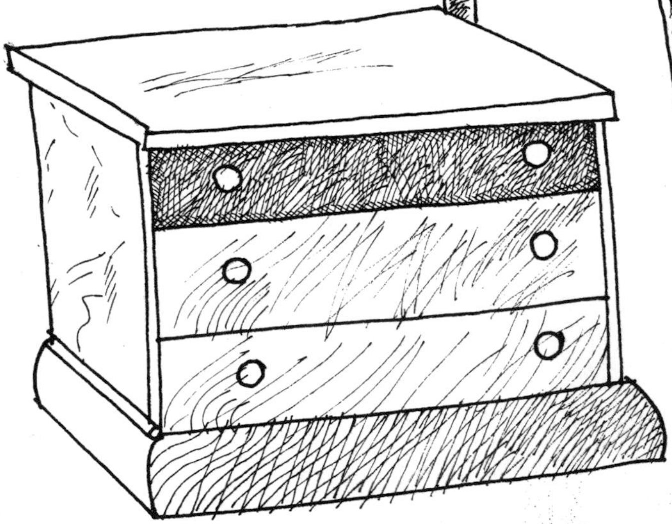

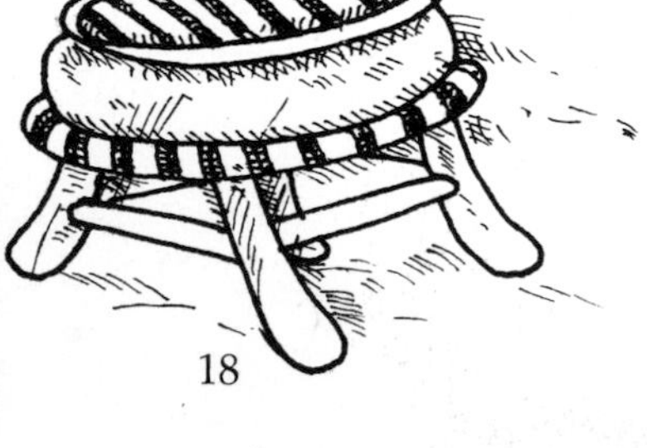

18

He was ...

He was ...
a boy who became
a man
a husband
a father.

He was ...
a good goalie,
a rotten batsman,
not bad at darts.

He was ...
second cornet in the works band;
a man who brought his pay-packet straight home,
without stopping at the pub;
a man who enjoyed his dinner.

He was ...
forgetful,
rarely on time,
sometimes tongue-tied,
at a loss for what to say.

He was ...
always honest,
never sober at Christmas,
often puzzled by the world.

He was ...
... my dad.

John Cunliffe

Shadow

The boy walks with his shadow
along the morning street.
The shadow of his body
is seen beyond his feet.

Like a slave the shadow is,
the boy its master. So
the two have always been
those many years ago

as far as history tells
and boys and girls walk by
over whatever street
under whatever sky.

But what if one fine day
the shadows should remain
after the boy and girl
have been forever gone?

Iain Crichton Smith

Bored

I'm ten and I'm bored
And I've nothing to do.
I'm fed up with watching
This ant on my shoe.

The Big Game has finished.
My brother won't play.
My dad says he won't let me
Watch *Match of the Day*.

I don't want to paint
Or to make model planes
Or to help Mum with cooking
Or to stroll country lanes.

I'm bored with my school,
With my books on the shelf,
And, most of all really,
Bored with being myself.

John Kitching

Blue Monday

Mondays I feel I'm useless,
That I'm no use at all —
A damp November firework;
A sad, split tennis ball;
A broken-handled cricket bat;
A rain-bedraggled tabby cat;
A liquid bowl of raspberry jelly,
A single, ancient, smelly welly.
Mondays I feel just useless.

Mondays I feel I'm hopeless —
A pip between the teeth;
A wrinkle in the bedclothes;
The wrestler underneath;
Some summer-soft and runny butter;
A Chinese torture dripping tap;
A blocked and flooded winter gutter;
A trap that's trapped inside a trap.
Mondays I feel just hopeless.

John Kitching

Half asleep

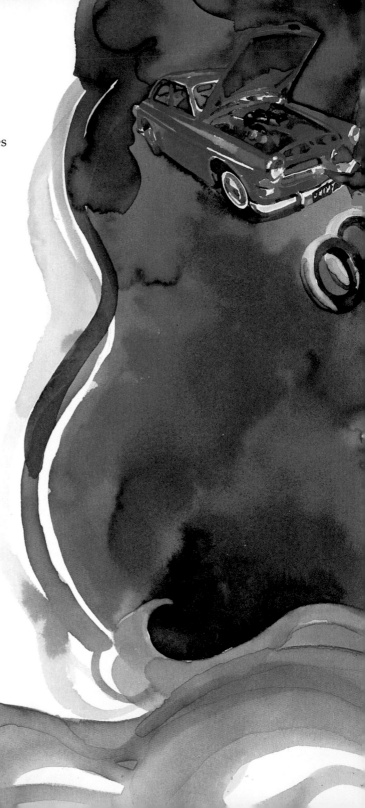

Half asleep
And half awake
I drift like a boat
On an empty lake
And the sounds in the houses
And street that I hear
Though far away
Sound very clear;
There's my sister Betty
Playing by the stairs
Shouting like teacher
At her teddy bears.

I can hear Mum chatting
To Mrs Spence next door
And I feel the tumbler
Vibrating the floor.
And Alan Simpson
Plays his guitar
And his dad
Keeps trying
To start his car.
Dave, the mechanic
Who's out on strike
Keeps tuning and revving
His Yamaha bike.
From the open window
Across the street
On the August air
Drifts a reggae beat.

At four o'clock
With a whoop and a shout
The kids from St. John's
Come tumbling out.
I can hear their shouts
Hear what they say
And I play in my head
All the games they play.

Gareth Owen

24

Cobble stone cobble stone

Cobble stone cobble stone,
Monkey on a wall
(Eight pence for a lemon)
Roll a plastic ball.

Cobble stone cobble stone,
Washing in the street
(Special offer toothpaste)
Slippers on his feet.

Cobble stone cobble stone,
In a flowered dress
(Green Shield Stamps)
She was shaped like an S.

John Kitching

You can't depend on anything

When I was just a little boy
I used to race about
and kick the empty rubbish tins
that people had left out.
I'm older
and know better now,
we learn things as we grow,
the tin that I just kicked was full
and nearly broke my toe.

Peggy Dunstan

I was mucking about in class

I was mucking about in class

Mr Brown said,
Get out and take your chair with me
I suppose he *meant* to say
Take your chair with you
so Dave said,
Yeah — you heard what he said
        get out and take my chair with him
so Ken said,
Yeah — get out and take his chair with me
so I said to Mr Brown
Yessir — shall I take our chair with you, sir?

Wow
That meant BIG TROUBLE

Michael Rosen

Not guilty

We have assembly every day
Assembly in the hall
And every day (or so it seems)
The Head, who's ten feet tall
(Or so it seems) has lots to say
About the writing on the wall.
And (so it seems) just every day
He looks at me with marbled eye
And makes me feel I wrote it all.
I go quite red from head to foot
(Or so it seems) and try to stare
Right back at him.
    'How do you dare,'
I want to shout, 'to make me feel
I wrote that stuff?' I'm more the type
Who'd look for rags to wipe
It out (or so it seems.)

John Kitching

The Loner

He leans against the playground wall,
Smacks his hands against the bricks
And other boredom-beating tricks,
Traces patterns with his feet,
Scuffs to make the tarmac squeak,
Back against the wall he stays —
And never plays.

The playground's quick with life,
The beat is strong.
Though sharp as a knife
Strife doesn't last long.
There is shouting, laughter, song,
And a place at the wall
For who won't belong.

We pass him running, skipping, walking,
In slow huddled groups, low talking.
Each in our familiar clique
We pass him by and never speak,
His loneness is his shell and shield
And neither he nor we will yield.

He wasn't there at the wall today,
Someone said he'd moved away
To another school and place
And on the wall where he used to lean
Someone had chalked
'watch this space.'

Julie Holder

The Stopper

Not in the regular team
But good for a kick-around
On a waste bit of ground
At the end of the street;
Never out of position
In opposition,
Hard and tall
And able to stop
The hottest shot
Without effort
And return the ball
With equal force;
Not great on attack
But the perfect back
That nothing gets past,
Whether slow or fast,
Angled, sliced,
Sidefooted,
Volleyed,
Bounced,
Or overhead;
Strong rather than clever
And apparently fit
To go on for ever —
That red brick wall
Against which you kick
Your ball.

Stanley Cook

The Commentator

Good afternoon and welcome,
This is Danny Markey your commentator
Welcoming you to this international
Between England and Holland,
Which is being played here this afternoon
At four Florence Terrace.
And the pitch looks in superb condition
As Danny Markey prepares
To kick off for England;
And this capacity crowd roars
As Markey, the England captain,
Puts England on the attack.
Straight away it's Markey
With a lovely pass to Keegan,
Keegan back to Markey,
Markey in possession now
Jinking skilfully past the dustbin
And a neat flick inside the cat there,
What a brilliant player this Markey is
And still only nine years old!
Markey to Francis,
Francis to Markey,
Markey is through . . .
No, he's been tackled by the drainpipe;
But he's won the ball back brilliantly
And he's advancing on the Dutch keeper now,
It must be a goal,
He comes off his line
But Markey chips him brilliantly
It's a goal . . .
No.
It's gone into Mrs Spence's next door.
And Markey's going round
To ask for his ball back.
The Crowd is silent now.
If he can't get the ball back
It could be the end of this international.
And now the door's opening
And yes, it's Mrs Spence,
Mrs Spence has come to the door,

And wait a minute, she's shaking her head,
She is shaking her head,
She is not going to let Markey
Have his ball back.
What is the referee going to do?
Markey looks very dejected here,
He's walking back, hanging his head ...
What's he doing now?
He seems to be waiting
And my goodness me
He's going back,
Markey is going back for the ball,
What a brilliant and exciting move;
He waited until the front door was closed
And then went back for that lost ball.
He's searching now,
He's searching for that ball
Down there by the compost heap
And wait a minute,
He's found it!
He's found that ball
And that's marvellous news
For the hundred thousand fans gathered here,
Who are showing their appreciation
In no uncertain fashion.
But wait a minute,
The door's opening once more;
It's her, it's Mrs Spence!
And she's waving her fist
And shouting something
But I can't make out what it is.
She's obviously not pleased.
And Markey's off,
He's running round in circles
Dodging this way and that
With Mrs Spence in hot pursuit,
And he's past her,
What skills this boy has.

But Mr Spence is here too
And Bruce their dog,
Markey is going to have to
Pull out something extra
To get out of this one;
He's only got Mr Spence and the bassett
To beat now. He's running straight at him.
And he's down, he's down on all fours;
What is he doing?
And Oh my goodness
That is brilliant,
That is absolutely brilliant,
He's gone between Spence's legs.
But he's got him,
This rugged tackler has got him,
He's got him by the jacket,
And Bruce is in there too,
Bruce has him by the seat of the pants,
He'll never get out of this one.
But he has,
He has got away;
He wriggled out of his jacket
And left part of his trousers with Bruce;
This boy is absolute dynamite.
He's over the wall, he's clear,
They'll never catch him now,
He's on his bike and
Through the front gate
And I don't think we'll see any more of Markey
Till the coast's clear
And it's safe to come home;
So this is Danny Markey ...
Handing you back to the studio.

Gareth Owen

Problem page from a women's magazine

Dear Maureen,
I am a lamp-post.
Every Saturday evening at five o'clock
three boys
wearing blue and white scarves
blue and white hats
waving their arms in the air
and shouting,
come my way.
Sometimes they kick me.
Sometimes they kiss me.
What should I do
to get them to make up their minds?
Yours bewilderedly,
Annie Onlight.

Michael Rosen

It isn't every day you see

It isn't every day you see
A wardrobe stuck inside a door;
A man was trying to shake it free;
He struggled till his hands were sore.

'I'll give a hand,' I said to him,
And, one each side, we heaved and strained;
We struggled for an hour until
All energy and strength were drained.

'Oh dear,' I gasped, 'I'll have to go;
It's stuck so tight we could take days
To get this blessed wardrobe out.'
He fixed me with a mournful gaze.

'Did you say, "Out"?' he said at last,
Rasping his fingers on his chin.
'You're trying to get this wardrobe out?
I'm trying to get it in.'

Gregory Harrison

KAHALACAHOO

36

I was going to see my Uncle Harry and I was standing on a station when I heard this announcement

The train now standing
at Flatworm's heaven
will not stop or start
at Oldham, Newham
You bring 'em, We buy 'em,
and all stations to
Kahalacahoo, Hawaii.

All messengers for
Upshot, Caughtshort
Stick'em up and Hijack
should travel in the slow coaches
at the rear of the train.

All passengers with messages
for Uncle Harry's cabbages
should stake their seats
in quicker coaches
now that Uncle Harry's cabbages
need weeding out
and watering.

Michael Rosen

The Haunted Lift

On the ground floor
of this ultramodern
tower block

in the dead
middle
of the night

the lift doors
open, with a
clang.

Nobody enters,
and nobody
comes out.

In the dead
middle
of the night

the lift doors
close with a clang,
and the lift begins

to move
slowly
up ...

with nobody in it,
nobody but
the ghost of a girl

who lived here once
on the thirteenth floor of
this ultramodern tower block.

One day, she went to play
in an old part of town,
and never came back.

She said she was just
going to the corner shop,
but she never came home.

Now her ghost
keeps pressing
in the dead

middle of the night
the button
for the thirteenth floor.

But when the door
opens with a clang
she cannot step out.

She gazes longingly
at the familiar landing,
but only for a moment ...

then the lift doors
clang in her face
and her tears

silently flow
as the lift
in the dead

middle
of the night
so soft and slow

carries her down again
down below,
far, far below

the ground
floor, where nobody
waits for the haunted lift

in the dead
middle
of the night.

Sometimes
on the thirteenth floor
her mother and father

with her photo
beside their bed
wake up

in the dead
middle of the night, and hear
the mysterious clanging

of closing lift doors,
and wonder
who it could be

in the dead
middle
of the night

using the lift
at such
an unearthly hour.

In this ultramodern
tower block
there is no thirteenth floor.

James Kirkup

The Grebs ...

When at night in bed I sleep
I hear the grebs around me creep,
I hear their whiskers scrape the floor,
I hear their fingers at the door.

I see their eyes shine in the dark,
I hear them squeal, I hear them bark.
'Oh Grebs, if you'll just go away,
I'll be good tomorrow, all day!'

But voices say 'Too late, too late!
We want you dead or alive!'
I tremble, shiver, shake and quiver
And beneath the bedclothes hide.

And feet and whiskers round me run
And closer, closer, closer come ...
'Oh Grebs, if you'll just go away,
I'll be good tomorrow, all day!'

'Too late,
Too late,
We're here...'

Mike Harding

Fingummy ...

Fingummy's fat
And Fingummy's small,
And Fingummy lives
With the boots in the hall.

If Fingummy bites,
If Fingummy tears,
If Fingummy chases you
Up the stairs

Shout 'Bumble-Bee Soup
And Bluebottle Jam.'
And run up to bed as fast as you can!

Cos Fingummy lives
Where there's never no light
And Fingummy makes
The dark sounds of the night,
And Fingummy's fat
And Fingummy's small
And Fingummy lives
In the dark, in the hall ...

Mike Harding

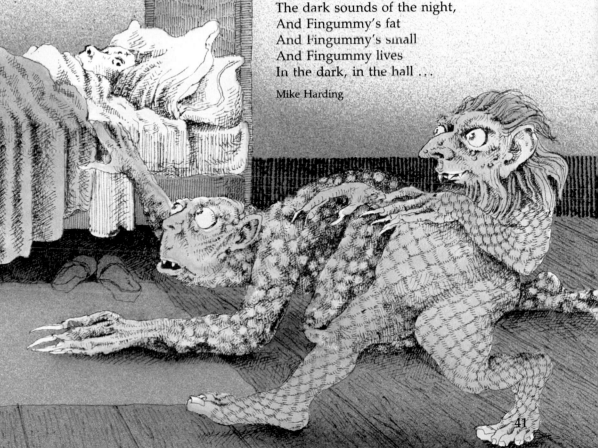

Nothing

He thought he heard
A footstep on the stair,
'It's nothing,' he said to himself,
'Nothing is there.'
He thought then he heard
A snuffling in the hall,
'It's nothing,' he said again,
'Nothing at all.'
But he didn't open the door
In case he found nothing
Standing there,
On foot or tentacle or paw.
Timidly quiet he kept to his seat
While nothing stalked the house
On great big feet.
It was strange though
And he'd noticed this
When on his own before,
Nothing stalked throughout the house
But never through his door.
The answer he thought,
Was very plain. It was because there was nothing there —
Again!

Julie Holder

The Diploblast

The Diploblast
Is always the last
To get up of an evening,
He scratches his head
Then goes back to bed
Which is why no one ever sees him.

Mike Harding

The Blob

And ... and what is it like?

> Oh, it's scary and fatbumped
> and spike-eared and groany.
> It's hairy and face-splumped
> and bolshie and bony.

And ... and where does it live?

> Oh, in comets and spaceships
> and pulsars and blackholes.
> In craters and sheepdips
> and caverns and northpoles.

And ... and what does it eat?

> Oh, roast rocks and fishlegs
> and x-rays and mooncrust.
> Then steelmeat and sun-eggs
> and lava and spacedust.

And ... and who are its enemies?

> Oh, Zonkers and Moonquakes
> and Sunquarks and Zigbags.
> Dumb Duncers and Milkshakes
> and Smogsters and Wigwags.

And ... and what does it wear?

> Not a thing! It's bare!

Wes Magee

The Dinosaur

Often I think of the dinosaur
like a tall ladder
racing about the world

with his small reptile head,
his small cruel eye,
his snake body.

But somewhere up above him,
high in a towering tree,
little man makes faces,

funny little man
who will one day walk
about the endless spaces

and build stone monuments
and create great paintings
even dinosaurs cannot eat.

Iain Crichton Smith

The Bogeyman

In the desolate depths of a perilous place
the bogeyman lurks, with a snarl on his face.
Never dare, never dare to approach his dark lair
for he's waiting … just waiting … to get you.

He skulks in the shadows, relentless and wild
in his search for a tender, delectable child.
With his steely sharp claws and his slavering jaws
oh he's waiting … just waiting … to get you.

Many have entered his dreary domain
but not even one has been heard from again.
They no doubt make a feast for the butchering beast
and he's waiting … just waiting … to get you.

In that sulphorous, sunless and sinister place
he'll crumple your bones in his bogey embrace.
Never never go near if you hold your life dear,
for oh! … what he'll do … when he gets you!

Jack Prelutsky

The Troll

Be wary of the loathsome troll
that slyly lies in wait
to drag you to his dingy hole
and put you on his plate.

His blood is black and boiling hot,
he gurgles ghastly groans.
He'll cook you in his dinner pot,
your skin, your flesh, your bones.

He'll catch your arms and clutch your legs
and grind you to a pulp,
then swallow you like scrambled eggs —
gobble! gobble! gulp!

So watch your steps when next you go
upon a pleasant stroll,
or you might end in the pit below
as supper for the troll.

Jack Prelutsky

Hello Mr Python

Hello Mr Python
Curling round a tree,
Bet you'd like to make yourself
A dinner out of me.

Can't you change your habits
Crushing people's bones?
I wouldn't like a dinner
That emitted fearful groans.

Spike Milligan

Hippoportant Poem . . .

A hippopotamus
Would squash a lot of us
If it sat on us.

Mike Harding

He's Behind Yer

'HE'S BEHIND YER!'
chorused the children
but the warning came too late.

The monster leaped forward
and fastening its teeth into his neck,
tore off the head.

The body fell to the floor
'MORE' cried the children,
'MORE'.

Roger McGough

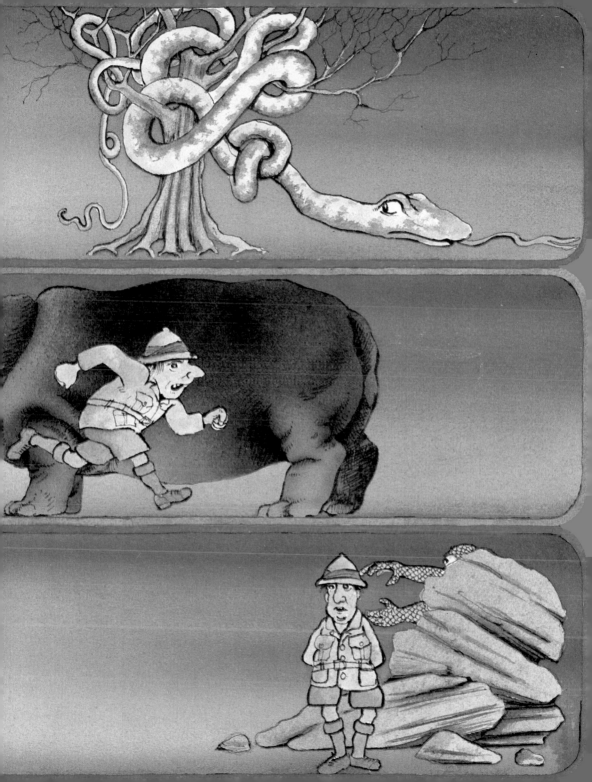

It makes a change

There's nothing makes a Greenland Whale
Feel half so high-and-mighty
As sitting on a mantelpiece
In Aunty Mabel's nighty.

It makes a change from Freezing Seas,
(Of which a Whale can tire),
To warm his weary tail at ease
Before an English fire.

For this delight he leaves the sea,
(Unknown to Aunty Mabel),
Returning only when the dawn
Lights up the Breakfast Table.

Mervyn Peake

The Silver Fish

While fishing in the blue lagoon,
I caught a lovely silver fish,
And he spoke to me, 'My boy,' quoth he,
'Please set me free and I'll grant your wish:
A kingdom of wisdom? A palace of gold?
Or all the fancies your mind can hold?'
And I said, 'OK', and I set him free,
But he laughed at me as he swam away,
And left me whispering my wish
Into a silent sea.

Today I caught that fish again
(That lovely silver prince of fishes),
And once again he offered me,
If I would only set him free,
Any one of a number of wishes
If I would throw him back to the fishes.

He was delicious.

Shel Silverstein

The Sea

Today the sea is playful and
casts a white froth across the sand
like the flounces on a long blue gown
which is shifting gently up and down.

Who would think that it would rage
like a great giant in a cage
swallowing sailor, ship and boat
and sucking them swiftly down its throat?

Iain Crichton Smith

Pirate

Like a cliff
My brow hangs over
The cave of my eyes
My nose is the prow of a ship

I plunder the world

Samuel Menashe

Pirate Captain Jim

'Walk the plank,' says Pirate Jim.
'But Captain Jim, I cannot swim.'
'Then you must steer us through the gale.'
'But Captain Jim, I cannot sail.'
'Then down with the galley slaves you go.'
'But Captain Jim I cannot row.'
'Then you must be the pirate's clerk.'
'But Captain Jim I cannot work.'
'Then a pirate captain you must be.'
'Thank you, Jim,' says Captain Me.

Shel Silverstein

53

Here, it is black, like the leeches and weeds,
And the bats flitting through the dank air.

It's just the same if I shut my eyes:
My companions, all around,
Are trickles, drips, sploshes, sudden *plops*.
Then, a strange, sucking sound.

One shoe's full of the cold dark water,
My hands slither over the stones.
My throat's gone dry, my heart pound-pounds,
but I can only go on —

Till I can see them, they can see me
and again they start to shout,
The rats bite, watch out for the rats.
But now I am almost out:

Dizzy, happy, I blink at the light.
The sun's still shining, the birds still sing.
Someone is patting me on the back —
Now I am one of the gang.

Brian Lee

The Tree House

It was an oak that defended a flowery bank
And spread its leaf-covered branches wide,
Waiting for a favourable wind
To sail across the river idling by.

The few small shoots on the trunk had broken off
Till the oak was almost impossible to climb
And the shoots were reduced to knuckles of wood
By the scrabbling feet of those who tried.

The cattle who scratched there polished the footholds,
The lowest branches were out of jump from the ground,
The oak was a century too old
For anyone to stretch his arms around.

There wasn't a fence or another tree for a ladder
Or cables of ivy tying the trunk up,
But they climbed on each other's shoulders
And somehow someone did it and let down a rope.

There in the long summer afternoons
They built and occupied their home from home
And though in a place where people seldom came
They were able to hide from them just the same.

Stanley Cook

Treasure Hunt

The first one, left behind the clock,
Said: *Walk down to the five-bar gate*
But do not open it. Between
One rusted hinge and the warped post,
The second message will be seen.

— We went down to the gate, and drew
A wisp of paper (faintly inked
With lines of writing) from the gap
Between the upright and the hinge;
And what it said was: *Read the map*

To find out where you are, then trace
A path uphill across the fields
Beyond this gate where you now stand,
Follow this track for half a mile,
Go round a wheat field to some land

Planted with conifers, then read
The first floor you can find. — And yet
We saw no 'floor' there, just a brick
Shelter with peep-holes, gloomy, damp,
Abandoned, overgrown. My stick

Scraped at the ground inside, and touched
A sack, barbed wire, and some dead leaves.
But when we stirred these leaves we read
Our third clue, scrawled in yellow chalk
On the cold concrete! This one said:

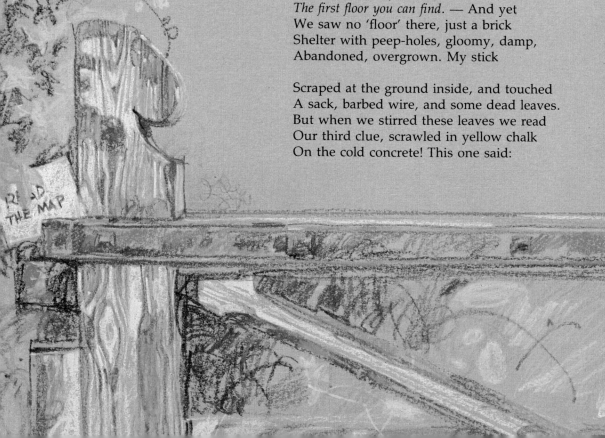

St. Mark's, the ruins, half-past four.
— In the noon sun we pored upon
The detail of the map. We knew
That we had passed no ruins, so
They lay ahead.... What could we do

But slog ahead for several miles,
Finishing all the food we had,
Until, well after three, we came
To a small valley where a church
Lay ruined in a field. The name

Was clear upon the map: 'St. Mark's.'
But where to find the clue? We searched
Among the ruins, nave and tower
And shattered porch, and scanned each inch
Three times, for what seemed like an hour

And then, at half-past four, the sun
Struck through one window-slit onto
A loosened stone in a flint wall.
Behind it, words had been scratched out
In the dark cavity, though all

They said was: *Row up to the lake.*
— There was one river, which ran off
The map too soon. But if the word
Was 'up', then it must mean 'upstream'.
In fact, we would have far preferred

An easier task than searching for
A river, boat, and oars, to fight
The current for what seemed a year,
But this we somehow did; and tried
To tell ourselves our prize was near,

And pulled, and tugged, against the stream,
And reached the lake! Just as night fell,
We drew in by a wharf, and saw
A scroll nailed to the planks, and read
This message as we slumped on shore:

You are to go back to the house.
Look at the map, and double back
To find a clue (the last, no doubt?)
In the last place and in the first,
The room from which you started out.

— By torchlight, and when torches failed,
By matchlight flames that flared and died
In seconds, we trudged all the way
Back. And by starving moonlight came
To where we had begun our day.

The gate stood open, and the door,
A meal was set for us to eat,
And eat we did! It was quite late
Before we thought again, and found
This note, left underneath my plate:

Look, just once more, behind the clock.
— We felt behind the clock, and there
(With fury and despair) we found:
Sleep through this night, get up at dawn,
And seek your prize on different ground.

We wondered, would we rise at dawn
And find a message sending us
To trace that circle round once more?
That was our fear as we lay down
To sleep that night. But what we saw

In the frail light of dawn was this:
Our treasure, waiting in the yard,
Tied up with tape and wax and string,
Taller than us and twice as wide,
So large it might be anything.

And if we told you what it was
We found when we unwrapped that box,
All it would do is let you see
The gift *we* longed for, searched for, won!
— And such a treasure might not be

The prize that *you* would want at all.
All hopes and dreams are different,
And since our prize might even fail
To interest you, I think we'll leave
The box untouched. And let you choose

Your own best ending to this tale.

Alan Brownjohn

Camping Pie

The wind roared up
And the sea boiled up
And the clouds piled up
And the storm built up
And the tents fell down.

And the lightning flashed
And the thunder crashed
And the heavy rain splashed
And the field turned brown.

And the sleeping bags swam
With the tea-bags and spam,
Crabs crawled in the wellies
And the pillows were wet jellies
And the sweaters in the drink
Began to shrink and shrink
And every pair of woolly socks did drown.

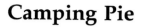

Then the wind died down
And the sea calmed down
And the storm wound down
And the sun shone down
From a clear blue sky.

Then all the buns and beans,
Sweating cheese and dripping jeans,
Muddy sandwiches and babies,
Soggy dogs and damp old ladies,
Sheep in unravelled flocks
And all the limp dead socks
Were put to dry.

And the wet field gleamed
And the birds all preened
And the hot sun beamed
And everything steamed.
That's camping pie.

Julie Holder

61

Lizzie and the Apple Tree

Once upon a time,
Every day for a while,
Lizzie sat up in the apple tree
Behind the leaves
And a smile,

And she said when they called
That she wouldn't come down
Till the apples dropped off
And the leaves turned brown.

She swung her legs
And laughed at their frown
And didn't come down
Didn't come down.

Lizzie sat up in
The apple tree's hair
In the wind and the rain
In the sun and the air.

Lizzie swung in
the apple tree's arms
And ignored her family's
Tempers and charms,

When Lizzie turned into an apple
They ceased to scold and berate her
And when the apples fell down
They forgot she was Lizzie —
And ate her!

Julie Holder

The Day

The breeze unpacks
The silken parachutes
From the bristled sack
Of the dried up thistle.

It teases the seeds apart
From the cotton wool of the willowherb
And the woodside smokes
With the millions of seeds afloat.

Warm air unpicks the pincushion
Of the dandelion
And plucks the tiny plume
From the head of the groundsel.

This is the day
Of the airborne invasion
With flower seeds parachuted
Into their future.

Stanley Cook

63

The Golden Boy

In March he was buried
    And nobody cried
Buried in the dirt
    Nobody protested
Where grubs and insects
    That nobody knows
With outer-space faces
    That nobody loves
Can make him their feast
    As if nobody cared.

But the Lord's mother
    Full of her love
Found him underground
    And wrapped him with love
As if he were her baby
    Her own born love
She nursed him with miracles
    And starry love
And he began to live
    And to thrive on her love.

He grew night and day
    And his murderers were glad
He grew like fire
    And his murderers were happy
He grew lithe and tall
    And his murderers were joyful
He toiled in the fields
    And his murderers cared for him
He grew a gold beard
    And his murderers laughed.

With terrible steel
　　They slew him in the furrow
With terrible steel
　　They beat his bones from him
With terrible steel
　　They ground him to powder
They baked him in ovens
　　They sliced him on tables
They ate him they ate him
　　They ate him they ate him.

Thanking the Lord
Thanking the Wheat
Thanking the Bread
For bringing them Life
Today and Tomorrow
Out of the dirt.

Ted Hughes

Leaves

Who's killed the leaves?
Me, says the apple, I've killed them all,
Fat as a bomb or a cannonball.
I've killed the leaves.

Who sees them drop?
Me, says the pear, they will leave me all bare,
So all the people can point and stare.
I see them drop.

Who'll catch their blood?
Me, me, me, says the marrow, the marrow,
I'll get so rotund that they'll need a wheelbarrow.
I'll catch their blood.

Who'll make their shroud?
Me, says the swallow, there's just time enough
Before I must pack all my spools and be off.
I'll make their shroud.

Who'll dig their grave?
Me, says the river, with the power of the clouds
A brown deep grave I'll dig under my floods.
I'll dig their grave.

Who'll be their parson?
Me, says the crow, for it is well-known
I study the bible right down to the bone.
I'll be their parson.

Who'll be chief mourner?
Me, says the wind, I will cry through the grass,
The people will pale and go cold when I pass.
I'll be chief mourner.

Who'll carry the coffin?
Me, says the sunset, the whole world will weep
To see me lower it into the deep.
I'll carry the coffin.

Who'll sing a psalm?
Me, says the tractor, with my gear grinding glottle
I'll plough up the stubble and sing through my throttle.
I'll sing the psalm.

Who'll toll the bell?
Me, says the robin, my song in October,
Will tell the still gardens the leaves are over.
I'll toll the bell.

Ted Hughes

Halloween

At night we walked the street.
I was wearing my wolf face.

The moon was shining brightly
and I began to howl.

The moon was like a plate.
I howled like a hungry wolf.

I howled and howled and howled,
till I met the lion.

Mask to mask we stood,
and our hair bristled.

Iain Crichton Smith

Halloween

'Granny, I saw a witch go by,
I saw two, I saw three!
I heard their skirts go swish, swish, swish —'

   'Child, 'twas leaves against the sky,
   And the autumn wind in the tree.'
'Granny, broomsticks they bestrode,
Their hats were black as tar,
And buckles twinkled on their shoes —'

   'You saw but shadows on the road,
   The sparkle of a star.'

'Granny?'
         'Well?'
'Don't you believe —?'
         'What?'
'What I've seen?
Don't you know it's Halloween?'

Marie Lawson

Recipe

If I tell you this tale you might wince,
It concerns an odd mixture for mince,
Made from dogs' teeth and tails
By a witch from North Wales
In a pot with a pattern of chintz.
You take pigs' ears and lemons and cheese,
And the wings and the stings from queen bees,
Some frogs live and frisky,
A cupful of whisky,
Some slugs and a few black-eyed peas.
Boil it an hour or two,
Season with essence of shrew;
If it turns out too salty,
The frogs must be faulty —
There's nothing at all you can do
(Except throw out the whole beastly brew!)

Shelagh McGee

Two Witches

There was a witch
The witch had an itch
The itch was so itchy it
Gave her a twitch.

Another witch
Admired the twitch
So she started twitching
Though she had no itch.

Now both of them twitch
So it's hard to tell which
Witch has the itch and
Which witch has the twitch.

Alexander Resnikoff

Bonfire

There's a great wild beast in my garden
   roaring and surging,
grinding his fierce, gold teeth
   under the trees
where the ground is crinkled and quilted
   with last year's leaf.

I can see his breath through the branches
   floating and climbing
into the calm, cool sky,
   and now and again
if I watch I can see him winking
   an angry eye.

Glinting and plunging he tears
   old paper and boxes
and swallows them till
   he is hungry no longer
but sleeps in a flutter of ashes,
   his sharp tongues still.

Jean Kenward

A Box of Fireworks

Silver Rain

Our gentlest fire,
soft as a house with foam walls,
it paints the damp grass silver
    where its rain falls.

Jumping Jack

This is the wild one
    (LOOK OUT!)
unpredictable as Brian Clough
    (CAREFUL!)
and a real eater of toes.

It goes mad at the lick of a flame
    (STAND BACK!)
and is a distant cousin
    (STEADY!)
of the Mercurian Glass-hopper.

Like a crackle of rifle-fire
    (WATCH IT!)
it leaps through the night
    (RUN! IT'S COMING!)
seeking you out.

Scatter!
Run!
It's got the scent
of your wellington boots!

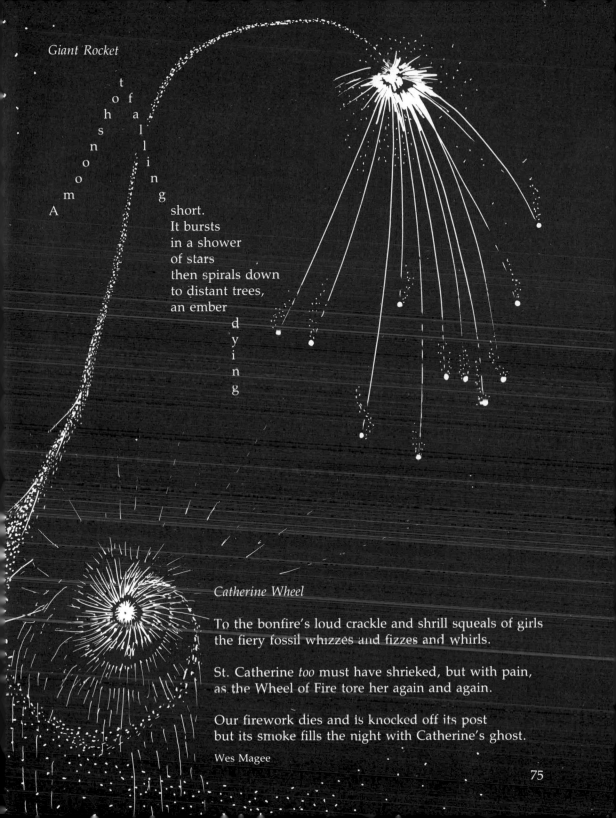

Giant Rocket

A
   m
  o
 o
  h
    s
     t
      o
       f
        a
         l
         l
          i
          n
          g

short.
It bursts
in a shower
of stars
then spirals down
to distant trees,
an ember

     d
     y
     i
     n
     g

Catherine Wheel

To the bonfire's loud crackle and shrill squeals of girls
the fiery fossil whizzes and fizzes and whirls.

St. Catherine *too* must have shrieked, but with pain,
as the Wheel of Fire tore her again and again.

Our firework dies and is knocked off its post
but its smoke fills the night with Catherine's ghost.

Wes Magee

November Night

Listen ...
With faint dry sound,
Like steps of passing ghosts,
The leaves, frost-crisped, break from the trees
And fall.

Adelaide Crapsey

Clouds

Clouds come from time to time —
    and bring to men a chance to rest
    from looking at the moon.

Matsuo Basho

76

Beneath the moon

Beneath the moon there is a hill
And in that hill there is a hall
And in that hall there is a throne
And on that throne there sits a king
And in his hand a crystal ball
And in that ball there shines a moon
And beneath that moon there is a hill
And in that hill there is a hall
And in that hall there is a throne
And on that throne ...

Mike Harding

The Blacksmith and The King

A rough day in winter, King Alfred commanded
All trades in his kingdom to gather together,
And he would decide which one was the greatest,
Did most for the people, met all their needs.

They came, those skilled craftsmen from the shires and the cities,
Bringing their tools and what they had made with them,
Packed the great hall of the palace with boasting,
Arguments, disputes, but no secrets revealed.

The tailor presented the king with a fine coat,
Purple and gold, silver buttons, silk-lined,
Alfred wore it with pleasure, and at sunset declared,
'The tailor has won. His trade is the greatest.'

Pandemonium and shouting, but the great king had spoken,
An uncomfortable silence, then the blacksmith called out,
'You are wrong, my lord King, I'm the prince of all craftsmen;
I'll not work again until you accept this.'

Stormed out of the hall in very high temper,
Leaving the tailor to self-satisfied smirking,
And back to their shops went the grumbling craftsmen,
Complaining of Alfred, and cursing the blacksmith.

But the man kept his word, his forge remained silent,
The anvil went rusty, the hammers were dumb,
No flashing of sparks, no flames in the furnace,
And the end of the magic of iron and fire.

Soon the other trades quarrelled and furiously bickered,
Their tools needed mending and new ones were wanted,
They were all facing ruin, the customers desperate,
None more than the tailor whose scissors were broken.

They held many meetings, they prayed in the churches,
Consulted the witches, grew poorer and poorer,
And when the king's horse cast a shoe in the courtyard,
Appealed to the blacksmith who refused to replace it.

And so they decided they could stand it no longer,
Broke into the smithy, butcher, baker and mason,
Farmer, jeweller and tanner, shipwright and vintner,
Cutler and tailor, clockmaker, weaver.

O what confusion, O what frustration;
The jostling and banging grew louder and louder,
But not one succeeded for not one was a blacksmith,
Their tools were still useless, and new ones unmade.

They turned on the tailor who made for the doorway
But he upset the anvil while evading their handling,
Which then hit the ground with a mighty explosion,
And frightened them all, and drowned all their voices.

And at this fearful moment the gentle Saint Clement,
Good friend of all blacksmiths, protector and patron,
Came in with the smith, and calmly reported,
'The king has relented, reversed his bad judgement.'

So the smith was triumphant and again began working,
The anvil was righted, air sang in the bellows,
New shoes for the king's horse and tools for the craftsmen;
'I am,' said the blacksmith, 'the prince of them all.'

Now the tailor had hidden beneath the forge table,
He took out a knife and slashed the smith's apron,
And so to this day that apron is ragged,
Remembering the tailor, the smith wears no other

And praises St. Clement at his feast in the winter,
Tells the tale to his children, fills the hole of the anvil
With small grains of gunpowder, with one blow from his hammer,
Explodes it in memory of the old smith and king.

Leonard Clark

Legend

Spring left the wood like a splinter
From a tree. Summer stared at the grass.
Autumn waited till the leaves dropped dead
Then it was winter, winter, nothing but winter.
Inside the wood a gloom of moss.
In its icy sky a red
Sun hung around like an eyesore till the moon
Took up night patrol and left at dawn.

Carrying haversacks and antique maps
Hunters headed for the wood to search
The naked branches and the frosted weeds
For clues, for secret places to set traps,
For clearings to see by fire and torch
What kept it cold. Their deeds
Added little to the local archives:
They found nothing and lost their lives.

Since then nobody has visited the wood,
Nor will the locals talk of it
Except to say that once some hunters went
To seek a purpose in the cold, made
Fires and set traps and used knives to cut
The trees, how something must have sent
Them to their deaths because they hear
Them cry in anguish each night of the year.

Alan Bold

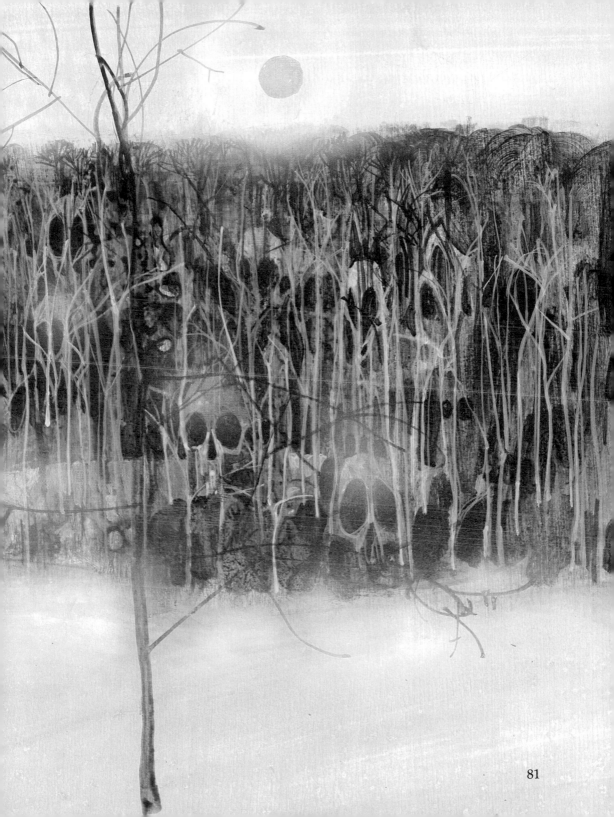

Week of Winter Weather

On Monday icy rains poured down
and flooded drains all over town.

Tuesday's gales rent elm and ash;
dead branches came down with a crash.

On Wednesday bursts of hail and sleet;
no one walked along our street.

Thursday stood out clear and calm
but the sun was paler than my arm.

Friday's frost that bit your ears
was cold enough to freeze your tears.

Saturday's sky was ghostly grey;
we smashed ice on the lake today.

Christmas Eve was Sunday and
snow fell like foam across the land.

Wes Magee

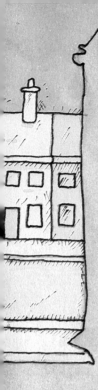

Carolling around the estate

The six of us met at Alan's house
  and Jane brought a carol sheet
that she got free from the butcher's shop
  when she bought the Sunday meat.

Jeremy had a new lantern light
  made by his Uncle Ted,
and Jim had 'borrowed' his Dad's new torch
  which flashed white, green, and red.

Our first call was at Stew Foster's place
  where we sang 'Three Kings' real well.
But his Mother couldn't stand the row
  and she really gave us hell!

We drifted on from door to door
  singing carols by lantern light.
Jane's lips were purple with the cold;
  my fingers were turning white.

Around nine we reached the chippie shop
  where we ordered pies and peas,
and with hot grease running down our hands
  we started to defreeze.

I reached home tired out, but my Mum said,
  'Your cousin Anne's been here.
She's carolling tomorrow night
  and I said you'd go, my dear.'

Wes Magee

Questions on Christmas Eve

But *how* can his reindeer fly without wings?
  Jets on their hooves? That's plain cheating!
And *how* can he climb down the chimney pot
  when we've got central heating?

You say it's magic and I shouldn't ask
  about Santa on Christmas Eve.
But I'm confused by the stories I've heard;
  I don't know what to believe.

I said that I'd sit up in bed all night long
 to see if he really would call.
But I fell fast asleep, woke up after dawn
 as something banged in the hall.

I saw my sock crammed with apples and sweets,
 and parcels piled high near the door.
Jingle bells tinkled far off in the dark;
 one snowflake shone on the floor.

Wes Magee

The Christmas Haiku

A Candle

That feather of flame
melting the window's ice skin
guides us through the night.

New Star

Atop the church spire
one hundred coloured bulbs flash
Christmas news in morse.

Christmas Bells

Urgent, they call us
across fields to a barn where
cows, a donkey stand.

Holly Sprig

Berries like blood drops,
and green leaves that remind us
Spring sleeps beyond the hill.

Robin

As heavy snow falls
he's a red-vested Batman
on the garden fence.

Wes Magee

Snowflakes

And did you know
That every flake of snow
That forms so high
In the grey winter sky
And falls so far,
Is a bright six-pointed star?
Each crystal grows
A flower as perfect as a rose.
Lace could never make
The patterns of a flake.
No brooch
Of figured silver could approach
Its delicate craftmanship. And think
Each pattern is distinct.
Of all the snowflakes floating there —
The million million in the air —
None is the same. Each star
is newly forged, as faces are,
Shaped to its own design
Like yours and mine.
And yet ... each one
Melts when its flight is done;
Holds frozen loveliness
A moment, even less;
Suspends itself in time —
And passes like a rhyme.

Clive Sansom

Snow for a week

The fields are piled;
The winter winds are cold and wild;
Across the yard the farmer goes,
Icicles hanging from his nose.
His load of fodder is so big
He wears it like a tangled wig;
And patient cattle wait to eat
A hay-stack walking on two feet.

Gregory Harrison

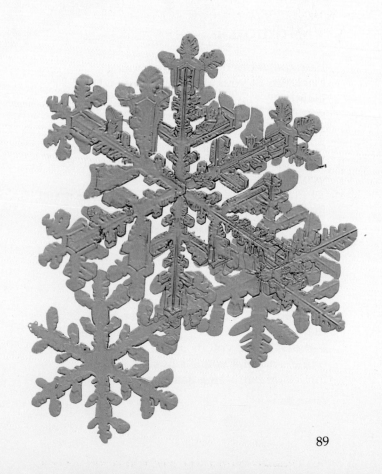

Small, smaller

I thought that I knew all there was to know
Of being small, until I saw once, black against the snow,
A shrew, trapped in my footprint, jump and fall
And jump again and fall, the hole too deep, the walls too tall.

Russell Hoban

Fieldmouse

I am too enormous for the gleaming
blackness of your beads of eyes to take in.
Unaware, you trickle right up to me,
searching for food.
               I lift my foot and you
drift under it, safe in the cool roofed dark.
You edge out. I put down a crumb close to
your etched front paws.
               At once you hug it and,
hunched up, begin to eat at starving speed,
fur grey and fine as ashes, shoulders bright
as an acorn.
            You devour the crumb and,
thistledown in a gentle breeze, you roll
satisfied to the haven of the hedge.

I'm glad you're as unaware of the hawk
that hunts you by day, of the phantasmal
owl that hunts you by night, as you are
of me, and that you live in such serene
innocence between a death and a death.

Albert Rowe

The Mole

Tube-dweller, he travels at speed
The main lines of the underground
Or starts branch lines beneath the fields,
Domed above by the earth he shovels out.

Dressed for the underground dirt and wet,
He lives in a twenty-four hour night
And could hardly tell the difference
Between darkness and light.

The whole of his life is spent in escaping
In tunnels he digs with his own two hands;
When the owl and the weasel hunt above ground,
The tunnels themselves mean freedom to him.

Stanley Cook

The Sparrow Hawk

Wings like pistols flashing at his sides,
Masked, above the meadow runway rides,
Galloping, galloping with an easy rein.
Below, the fieldmouse, where the shadow glides,
Holds fast the small purse of his life, and hides.

Russell Hoban

Owls

They stare at you,
these ugly phantoms of the night,
and do not seem to care
if you stare back at them.
All day they perch, half asleep,
in lonely ruins, dark church towers,
not liking the sun,
dozing, and dreaming with stupid face,
of scurrying mice, fat beetles, baby birds,
swallowed greedily in one cruel gulp.

At twilight they come out.
Like floating paper glide along lanes,
noiselessly dipping over hedges,
or fanning their ghostly way
around the houses, down the avenues,
ears and eyes set for the kill.
Then, gorged with fresh meat,
they sag back home,
the moon's eye watching them,
hooting in the wind,
waiting for the next raw victim.

I do not like owls.
I shiver when I hear them
screeching at the bottom of the garden,
invading the darkness,
glad I'm not a mouse,
small bird or beetle.

Leonard Clark

The Wolf Spider

Lurking among the grass-root knots
pounces a creature, merciless, cunning —
A spider with eight enormous hairy legs — oh —
It's as big as a wolf and it's running,
   running, running.

Not a web-spinner
which lies in wait for its dinner
Of flies which blunder and buzz
but a wolf spider
who runs down his prey
As the lone timber wolf does.

R. C. Scriven

Mosquito

At night
when I'm tucked tight in bed
you whine and dive
around my head.
You walk
  and stalk me
    up the sheet
with stick legs
bent up into feet.
There isn't any way you please
with elbows
where you should have knees —
and here's another horrid thing —
  you've got a sting.

Peggy Dunstan

A Hair-raising Experience

Once I saw two earwigs
  Sitting on a chair;
I looked into a mirror —
  And found my ears were bare . . .

Carey Blyton

My Dog

My dog is such a gentle soul,
  Although he's big it's true.
He brings the paper in his mouth.
  He brings the postman too.

Max Fatchen

The Clever Rabbit

There was a little rabbit
who was lying in his burrow
When the Dingo rang him up to say
he'd call on him tomorrow.

But the rabbit thought it better
that the Dingo didn't meet him
So he found another burrow
and the Dingo didn't eat him.

D. H. Souter

Old Hogan's Goat

Old Hogan's goat was feeling fine,
Ate six red shirts from off the line.
Old Hogan grabbed him by the back
And tied him to the railroad track.

Now as the train came into sight,
The goat grew pale and green with fright.
He heaved a sigh as if in pain,
Coughed up those shirts and flagged the train.

Anon.

Cyril the Centipede

Cyril the centipede
Loved playing games,
And his favourite one was football.
And when he played goal
With nine fleas and a mole
Nothing got past him at all.

They played spiders and newts
But his one hundred boots
Gave his team very little to do
And the fleas would get bored,
And the mole never scored
And the crowd would just stand there and boo.

Till one awful day the crowd stayed away
And no fans for either side came,
But all said and done
When it's none none none none,
It's not really much of a game.
Then Cyril the centipede
Hurt his back leg
The hundredth one down on the right
So he used a small stick
And went 99 click,
Now I'm happy to say it's all right.
But he doesn't play goal
Any more — he's retired
Unbeaten, for nobody scored.
Now he just referees
For the spiders and fleas,
And even the mole
Has just scored.

Jeremy Lloyd

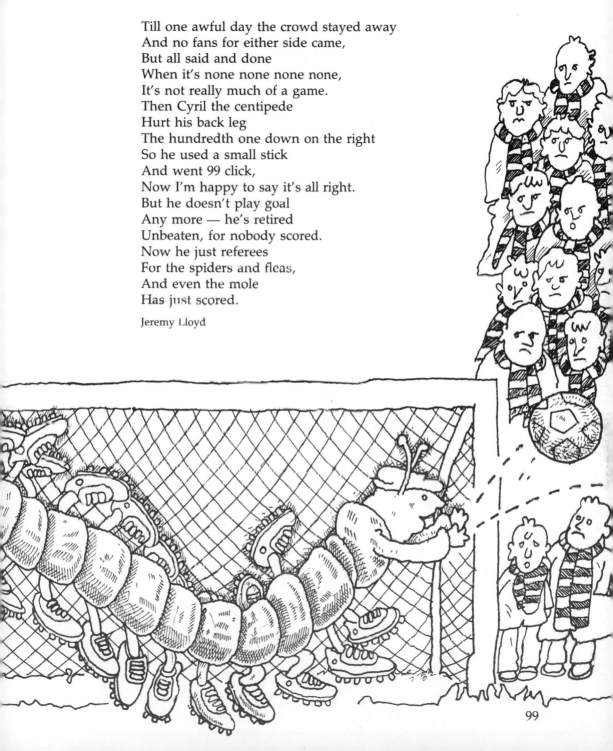

99

The Frog and the Ox

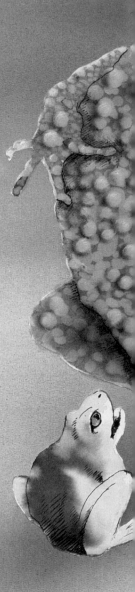

Two frogs
Sat croaking down a country lane
A plop-song with a croak refrain,
When — heavy, heedless how he came
Or where he trod — an ox swung by ...
One frog remained.

Mother Frog,
Splashing in her pool nearby,
Heard his piping piteous cry;
'Mother!
A dreadful beast obscured the sky.
His careless hoof has crushed my brother.
Hurry, hurry!'

Two splashes — three hops —
She leaps through the air and flops
Beside him, all froth and flurry:
'You ought to have stayed, as you were told,
Under the lush marsh-marigold —
But tell me, what was he like?'

'Four-legged he walked, with swishing tail and chewing chops
And magisterial slow mud-sucking pops.'
'As big as this?'
She puffed her portly figure
Into a speckled ball.
'Bigger.
That's far too small.'
She puffed and puffed her portly figure
Into a green balloon.
'Go on — you'll get there soon.'
She puffed and puffed and puffed her portly figure
Into a monster pumpkin, red as a fire.
'Fuller, fatter, broader, higher,
Thick as a barn and tall as a spire!'

With blow and bluster, vim and verve and vigour,
She puffed and puffed and puffed
   And puffed and puffed and puffed
      Until
         (Come what must)
         She B-U-S-T!

Ian Serraillier

Hannibal the Snail

Along the playground tarmac
Signing it with his trail,
Glides Hannibal the Hero
Hannibal the snail.

Under the burning sun
In the asphalt desert dust,
Hannibal with a placard
'TO THE FOOTBALL FIELD OR BUST!'

Spurning food or drink,
Refusing offers of aid,
Hannibal hurries slowly on
And won't be put in the shade.

His trail is snail miles long
Its silver is tarnished and dimming
But Hannibal shoulders his dusty shell
And points his horns to winning.

Triumphant he glides to the balm of the grass,
Into the cool of the clover,
Hannibal's crossed his desert
His impossible journey is over.

He slides through the dandelions
Exploring each stalk and stem byway
And could that be Hannibal singing
'I did it my way'?

Julie Holder

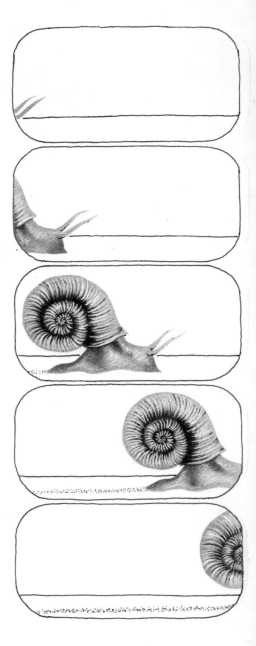

Silly Old Baboon

There was a baboon
Who, one afternoon,
Said, 'I think I will fly to the sun.'
So, with two great palms
Strapped to his arms,
He started his take-off run.

Mile after mile
He galloped in style
But never once left the ground,
'You're running too slow,'
Said a passing crow,
'Try reaching the speed of sound.'

So he put on a spurt —
By God how it hurt!
The soles of his feet caught fire.
There were great clouds of steam
As he raced through a stream
But he still didn't get any higher.

Racing on through the night,
Both his knees caught alight
And smoke billowed out from his rear.
Quick to his aid
Came a fire brigade
Who chased him for over a year.

Many moons passed by.
Did Baboon ever fly?
Did he ever get to the sun?
I've just heard today
That he's well on his way!
He'll be passing through Acton at one.

Spike Milligan

Bird and Boy

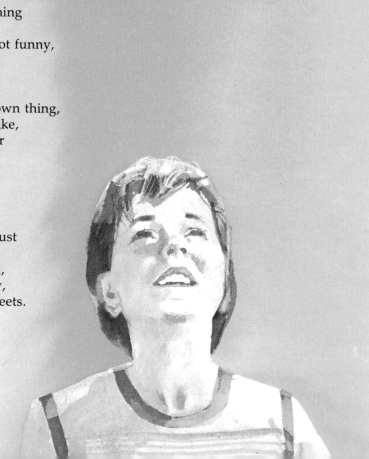

So you want to fly. Why?
  You haven't any feathers.
Do you think it's good fun
  Being out in all weathers?
Said Bird to Boy.

You haven't any wings,
  You can't build a nest.
Why aren't you satisfied.
  With the things you do best?
Said Bird to Boy.

What would it be like?
  A sky full of boys,
Their arms flapping, their big feet —
  And the noise!
Said Bird to Boy.

Have you ever tried perching
  In some old tree
When it's snowing? It's not funny,
  Believe me!
Said Bird to Boy.

Be comfortable, do your own thing,
  Your skateboard, your bike,
Your football, all the other
  Things you like.
    Why try to fly?
  Stay out of the sky,
Said Bird to Boy.

Yes, you're right, I can't just
  Flap my arms and fly.
But I dream about it often,
  Winging through the sky,
Above the houses, the streets.
  I'd like to try.
Said Boy to Bird.

Leslie Norris

Mr. Pennycomequick

Mr. Hector Pennycomequick
 Stood on the castle keep,
Opened up a carriage-umbrella
 And took a mighty leap.

'Hooray!' cried Mr. Pennycomequick
 As he went through the air.
'I've always wanted to go like this
 From here to Newport Square.'

But Mr. Hector Pennycomequick
 He never did float nor fly.
He landed in an ivy-bush
 His legs up in the sky.

Mr. Hector Pennycomequick
 They hurried home to bed
With a bump the size of a seagull's egg
 On the top of his head.

'So sorry,' said Mr. Pennycomequick,
 'For causing all this fuss.
When next I go to Newport Square
 I think I'll take the bus.'

The moral of this little tale
 Is difficult to refute:
A carriage-umbrella's a carriage-umbrella
 And not a parachute.

Charles Causley

Rockabye baby

Rockabye baby
  On the stairtop,
Crying and screaming
  When will she stop?
Is it her temper?
  The way that she's pinned?
Rockabye baby
  It's simply the wind.

Max Fatchen

Humpty Dumpty

Humpty Dumpty sat on a wall,
Humpty Dumpty had a great fall.
All the king's horses and all the king's men
Had scrambled eggs for breakfast again.

Anon.

Mary had a little lamb

Mary had a little lamb,
'Twas awful dumb, it's true.
It followed her in a traffic jam,
And now it's mutton stew.

Mary had a little lamb
As dirty as a hog.
They asked her how it got that way.
She answered simply, 'Smog.'

Mary had a little lamb,
Her father shot it dead.
Now Mary takes her lamb to school
Between two hunks of bread.

Anon.

There was a young fellow called Hugh

There was a young fellow called Hugh
Who went to a neighbouring zoo.
 The lion opened wide
 And said, 'Come inside
And bring all the family too.'

Max Fatchen

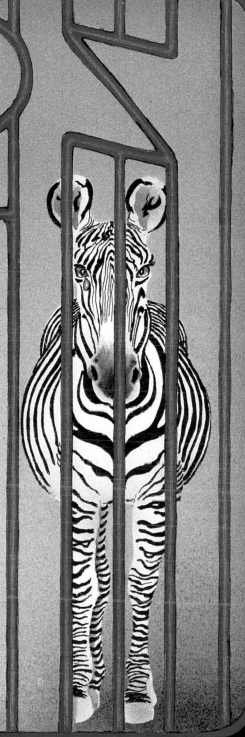

Norman the Zebra

Norman, a zebra at the zoo,
Escaped and ran to Waterloo
And caused a lot of consternation
In the rush-hour, at the station.
He had an awful lot of fun
Chasing folk on Platform 1,
And then he ran to Regent's Park
And hid there until it was dark,
And thought of his keeper Mr Prout,
How cross he'd be, that he'd got out.
So he tiptoed to the big zoo gate
And found he'd got there just too late.
Poor Norman had a little weep
And lay down in the road to sleep
And woke up early from his rest,
With people walking on his chest.
And someone said, 'I think that's new,
A zebra crossing near the zoo.'
And with a snort of indignation,
Regretting leaving for the station,
He cried, 'I've had enough of that,
How dare you use me as a mat.
I'm going straight home to the zoo.'
He was just in time for breakfast too.

Jeremy Lloyd

The Monkey and You

I am a monkey
In a zoo.
You stare at me
I stare at you.
If I swing by my tail,
Chatter, pull faces,
Go through the usual monkey paces,
Which I have learned
You consider your due,
Perhaps you'll throw me a peanut or two.

I am a monkey
In a zoo.
You stare at me
I stare at you.
You chatter, pull faces,
Hold out your hand,
You look intelligent enough
To make me think you understand
My monkey state
And are trying to communicate.

I am a monkey
In a zoo.
You stare at me
I stare at you.
Two sides to these bars there are.
What is life like over there
In your zoo?
At least you have peanuts to spare,
Who throws the peanuts to you?

Julie Holder

Bear

In wilds of old
the bear grew thin and ragged
as he lay in his cave,
dreaming of meat and honey,
of summer food and drink,
while out in the cold,
winter raged.

In zoos today,
the bear grows plump and melancholy,
the sun and warmth are there,
and food is brought
day by day,
while out in the cold,
the people stare.

Inger Hagerup and Joan Tate

Are you pleased with the donkey you bought at the fair?

'Are you pleased with the donkey you bought at the fair?'
I asked the old man with the flowing white hair.
'Oh yes, a fine beast. I've had him since March.
But that bridge is a nuisance.
His ears catch on the arch.
So,
I'm cutting some grooves for his ears in the stone,
But it takes a long time
When you're working alone.'

'It's none of my business,' I said with a smile,
But I had it in mind that it might be worth while
To dig out the path —
Less work don't you know.'

He thought for a minute and then answered slow,
'Ah, yes, but hold on, it's not how it appears;
He ain't long in the leg;
He's too long in the ears.'

Gregory Harrison

Old Man

There was an old man
who lived in our town,
as I grew up,
he grew down,

until he became
so crooked and small
there was nothing left
of him at all.

He shuffled along,
eyes fixed on the street,
only inches between
his head and feet.

When for the last time
the town saw him alive,
I had grown to a giant
of four foot five,

and he was a dwarf
with a wobbling head,
and a faraway voice,
but now he's dead.

Did they straighten him out
when he came to die
to fit his small coffin,
and where he will lie

beneath a tall tree,
tight under the ground,
and as hunchbacked as him
his little green mound?

Leonard Clark

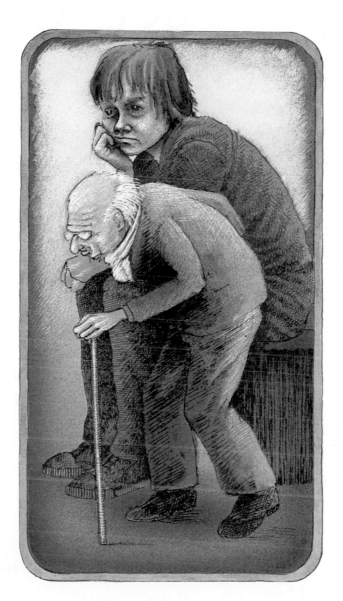

The Old Men

I heard the old, old men say,
'Everything alters,
And one by one we drop away.'
They had hands like claws, and their knees
Were twisted like the old thorn-trees
By the waters.
I heard the old, old men say,
'All that's beautiful drifts away
Like the waters.'

W. B. Yeats

114

Old Johnny Armstrong

Old Johnny Armstrong's eighty or more
  And he humps like a question-mark
Over two gnarled sticks as he shuffles and picks
  His slow way to Benwell Park.

He's lived in Benwell his whole life long
  And remembers how street-lights came,
And how once on a time they laid a tram-line,
  Then years later dug up the same!

Now he's got to take a lift to his flat,
  Up where the tall winds blow
Round a Council Block that rears like a rock
  From seas of swirled traffic below.

Old Johnny Armstrong lives out his life
  In his cell on the seventeenth floor,
And it's seldom a neighbour will do him a favour
  Or anyone knock at his door.

With his poor hands knotted with rheumatism
  And his poor back doubled in pain,
Why, day after day, should he pick his slow way
  To Benwell Park yet again? —

O the wind in park trees is the self-same wind
  That first blew on a village child
When life freshly unfurled in a green, lost world
  And his straight limbs ran wild.

Raymond Wilson

115

Figure in a Seascape

I saw this tired old woman
On the beach, picking stones,
And I knew her
Or thought I knew her.
She looked back on her years
Of resignation
With a certain satisfaction:
She had endured
Some of the stones heaped on her,
She had refused to collapse
Under the weight of it all.
She continued to pick stones,
To feel them in her fingers,
Feel them in her bones.
She stood still for a moment
Looking at the waves,
A ruin beside the sea.
She stood there aware
Of how her past
Had become her present.
White hair. Tawny beach. Clear skies.
And that faraway look in her eyes.

Alan Bold

High on the hill

High on the hill I can see it all,
the anthill men and the doll's house town,
the bowl of sea and the trim toy ships.
Here only the trees at hand are tall.

High on the hill I can touch a cloud
or measure miles with my fingertips,
can hide the town with a palm turned down
and drown its noise when I speak aloud.

High on the hill it's all a joke
and I wonder why I bothered at all
with the clockwork cars and the anthill folk
that height and distance make so small.

Tom Wright

I was told

That misty morning
they set up their banners on the hills,
charged into the valley with axes and spears;
the bowmen played havoc,
a thousand dead bodies left behind for the crows,
but who they all were and who won in the end,
I do not know;
only a few sheep are grazing there now.

That hot evening
heads of dragons rose up out of the lake
spouting fire, the sun red as blood;
the terrified villagers fled away to the woods,
many old people and babies left behind in their huts,
but who they all were and what happened in the end,
I do not know;
only a few frogs are swimming there now.

Leonard Clark

A Piece of Sky

There was this child,
Not very old,
Who looked at the sky
Blue pink and gold
And wanted a piece,
Just a pie-sized slice,
To hold.
He knew just how it would feel.
Treasure heavy it would weigh
And magic, it would change colour
With the day
From light to dark, from blue to grey.
He didn't want to keep it,
Just to borrow,
They could put it back again,
He said,
Tomorrow.
They questioned him with what and why.
The sky,
He said
Was like a dome that fitted the earth
Exactly half-way down.
It drew the horizon,
Outlined the trees,
Held down the mountains
And stemmed the seas.
And the tide?
Too many people on one side
Of the world,
East or West, South or North,
Tilted it and made the seas slop back and forth.
And cloud?
Cloud was fog on holiday.
And fog?
Fog was cloud, the other way.
And rainbows?
Rainbows were the ghosts of lights
That people switched off
In the middles of nights.
And ...?

He tired of questions
He was ready for bed
He didn't know everything he said.
Their questions really made him sigh
All he had wanted was a piece of sky.
They explained the world to him.
Told him the what and where and why
Of cloud and rainbows, sky and tide
Until he thought his brains were fried.
Then he smiled at them, politely sceptic
After all, their explanation of the world
Was too fantastic.

Julie Holder

Time

Yesterday is misty land
Far away with bandaged head
And hand held mother-tight
And monsters here and fled.

Today is grey country
Here and now and no escape
With sums and salt and bread
And too few hints of hope.

Tomorrow is another land
Far away and young and old
With mystery and spice and sun
And happy gold and happy gold.

John Kitching

Index of first lines

Acknowledgements

The following poems are appearing for the first time in this anthology and are reprinted by permission of the author unless otherwise stated.

Carey Blyton: 'A Hair-raising Experience'. © 1981 Carey Blyton. Alan Bold: 'Legend', 'Figure in a seascape'. Both © 1981 Alan Bold. Gyles Brandreth: 'Mr Ah Choo'. © 1981 Gyles Brandreth. Alan Brownjohn: 'Treasure Hunt'. © 1981 Alan Brownjohn. Leonard Clark: 'The Blacksmith and the King'. © 1981 Leonard Clark. Reprinted by permission of Robert Clark, Literary Executor. Stanley Cook: 'The Stopper', 'The Tree House', 'The Day' and 'The Mole'. All © 1981 Stanley Cook. John Cunliffe: 'He was...'. © 1981 John Cunliffe. Gregory Harrison: 'Snow for a week', 'It isn't every day you see', 'Are you pleased with the donkey you bought at the fair'. All © 1981 Gregory Harrison. Julie Holder: 'A Piece of Sky', 'The Alien', 'The Loner', 'Nothing', 'Camping Pie', 'Lizzie and the Apple Tree', 'Hannibal the Snail', and 'The Monkey and You'. All © 1981 Julie Holder. James Kirkup: 'The Haunted Lift'. © 1981 James Kirkup. Reprinted by permission of Dr. Jan Van Loewen Ltd. John Kitching: 'Time', 'Bored', 'Blue Monday', 'Cobble stone Cobble stone', and 'Not Guilty'. All © 1981 John Kitching. Wes Magee: 'The Mystery Creatures', 'Questions', 'The Blob', 'Week of Winter Weather', 'Carolling around the estate', 'Questions of Christmas Eve', 'The Christmas Haiku' and 'A Box of Fireworks'. All © 1981 Wes Magee. Michael Rosen: 'If your hands get wet', 'Once I was round a friend's place' and 'I was mucking about in class'. All © 1981 Michael Rosen. Albert Rowe: 'Fieldmouse'. © 1981 Albert Rowe. Ian Serraillier: 'The Frog and the Ox'. © 1981 Ian Serraillier. Ian Crichton Smith: 'The Sea'. © 1981 Iain Crichton Smith. Raymond Wilson: 'Old Johnny Armstrong'. © 1981 Raymond Wilson.

The Editor and Publisher wish to thank the following for permission to reprint copyright poems in this anthology. Although every effort has been made to contact the owners of the copyright in poems published here, a few have been impossible to trace. If they contact the Publisher, correct acknowledgement will be made in future editions.

Matsuo Basho: 'Clouds' from An Introduction to Haiku by Harold G. Henderson. Copyright © 1958 by Harold G. Henderson. Reprinted by permission of Doubleday & Company, Inc. Charles Causley: 'Mr. Pennycomequick' from Figgie Hobbin (Macmillan). Reprinted by permission of David Higham Associates Ltd. Leonard Clark: 'Owls', 'Old Man' and 'I Was Told', all from The Singing Time. Reprinted by permission of Hodder & Stoughton Children's Books. Peggy Dunstan: 'You can't depend on anything' and 'Mosquito', both from In and Out the Windows. Reprinted by permission of Hodder & Stoughton Children's Books. Max Fatchen: 'There was a young fellow called Hugh', 'Rockabye baby', 'My dog' and 'Why is it?', all from Songs For My Dog & Other People (Kestrel Books, 1980), pp.35, 54-55, 15, 44. Copyright © 1980 by Max Fatchen. Reprinted by permission of Penguin Books Ltd., and Winant, Towers Limited. Inger Hagerup: 'Bear', translated by Joan Tate, from Helter Skelter (Pelham Books). Reprinted by permission of Michael Joseph Ltd. Mike Harding: 'Beneath the Moon', 'Hippoportant Poem...', 'The Diploblast', 'The Grebs' and 'Fingummy', all from Up the Boo Aye Shooting Pookakies. © Moonraker Productions Limited 1980. Reprinted by permission. Russell Hoban: 'Small, smaller' and 'The Sparrow Hawk', both from The Pedalling Man © 1968. Reprinted by permission of World's Work Ltd., and Grosset & Dunlap, Inc. Ted Hughes: 'The Golden Boy' and 'Leaves', both from Season Songs. Copyright © 1968, 1973, 1975 by Ted

Hughes. Reprinted by permission of Faber & Faber Ltd., and Viking Penguin Inc. Jean Kenward: 'Eager & Stout' and 'Bonfire', both from *Old Mister Hotch-Potch*. Reprinted by permission of Thornhill Press. Marie A. Lawson: 'Halloween' from *Child Life Magazine*. Copyright 1936, 1964 by Rand McNally & Company. Reprinted by permission. Brian Lee: 'The Tunnel' from *Late Home* (Kestrel Books, 1976) p.10. Copyright © 1976 by Brian Lee. Reprinted by permission of Penguin Books Ltd. Jeremy Lloyd: 'Cyril the Centipede' and 'Norman the Zebra' both from *Captain Beaky*. Copyright © 1977 Captain Beaky Music Ltd. Administered throughout the world by Chappell Music Ltd. Reproduced by kind permission. Shelagh McGee: 'Recipe' from *Witches*. Reprinted by permission of Robson Books Ltd. Roger McGough: 'He's Behind Yer'. Reprinted by permission of A.D. Peters & Co. Ltd. Samuel Menashe: 'Pirate' from *To Open*. Copyright © 1961 by Samuel Menashe. Reprinted by permission of the author, and Viking Penguin Inc. Spike Milligan: 'Hello Mr. Python' from *Silly Verse for Kids*; 'Silly Old Baboon' from *A Book of Milliganimals*. Reprinted by permission of Dobson Books Limited. Leslie Norris: 'Bird and Boy' from *Stories and Rhymes* (BBC Publications, 1980). Reprinted by permission of the author. Gareth Owen: 'Half Asleep' and 'The Commentator' from *Stories and Rhymes* (BBC Publications, 1980). Reprinted by permission of the author. Mervyn Peake: 'It makes a change' from *Rhymes Without Reason* (Methuen Children's Books). Reprinted by permission of Eyre Methuen Ltd. Jack Prelutsky: 'The Bogeyman' and 'The Troll' both from *Nightmares: Poems to Trouble Your Sleep*. Text copyright © 1976 by Jack Prelutsky. Reprinted by permission of A. & C. Black Ltd., and Greenwillow Books (A Division of William Morrow & Co.). Alexander Resnikoff: 'Two Witches' from *Oh How Silly* (edited by William Cole, Eyre Methuen Ltd./Viking Press, Inc). Reprinted by permission of Laurence Pollinger Ltd. Michael Rosen: 'Problem Page from a Women's Magazine' and 'I was going to see my Uncle Harry...', both from *Wouldn't You Like to Know* (1977). Reprinted by permission of Andre Deutsch. Clive Sansom: 'Snowflakes' from *An English Year* (Chatto & Windus). Reprinted by permission of David Higham Associates Ltd. R.C. Scriven: 'The Wolf Spider' from *Stories and Rhymes* (BBC Publications, 1980). Reprinted by permission of the author. Shel Silverstein: 'Pirate Captain Jim' and 'Silver Fish' from *Where the Sidewalk Ends: The Poems and Drawings of Shel Silverstein*. Copyright © 1974 by Shel Silverstein. Reprinted by permission of Harper & Row, Publishers Inc. Iain Crichton Smith: 'Reflection', 'Shadow', 'The Dinosaur' and 'Halloween', all from *River, River*. Reprinted by permission of Macdonald Publishers, Edinburgh. D.H. Souter: 'The Clever Rabbit' from *Emu Stew* (ed. Patricia Wrighton). First published in *School Magazine* by the New South Wales Education Dept. Judith Thurman: 'Soap' from *Flashlight & Other Poems* (New York: Atheneum, 1976/Kestrel Books, 1977), p.32. Copyright © 1976 by Judith Thurman. Reprinted by permission of Atheneum Publishers, and Penguin Books Ltd. Kit Wright: 'Give up slimming, Mum' from *Rabbitting On* (Fontana Lions). Reprinted by permission of Fontana Paperbacks. Tom Wright: 'High on the hill' from *Delights and Warnings* (ed. J. & G. Beer). Reprinted by permission of the author. W.B. Yeats: 'The Old Men Admiring Themselves in the Water' from *Collected Poems* (Macmillan, London 1950/Macmillan, New York 1956). Reprinted by permission of A.P. Watt Ltd., for M.B. Yeats, Anne Yeats and Macmillan London Limited, and by permission of Macmillan Publishing Co., Inc. Anon: 'Mary had a little lamb', 'Humpty Dumpty' and 'Old Hogan's Goat' are reprinted by permission of Sterling Publishing Co., Inc., New York, from *Silly Verse (and even worse)* by Joseph Rosenbloom. © 1979 by Joseph Rosenbloom.

The publishers would like to thank the following for permission to reproduce photographs:

Ardea, p. 111; Barnaby's Picture Library, pp. 82–3; Bruce Coleman, pp. 76–7, 88–9; Richard and Sally Greenhill, pp. 26, 27, 54, 55; Frank Lane Agency, p. 117; John Topham Picture Library, pp. 63, 66–7; Burke Uzzle/Magnum p. 23; John Walmsley, pp. 30, 31 (details).